Science Inquiry
WHAT DO
ANIMALS NEED
TO SURVIVE?

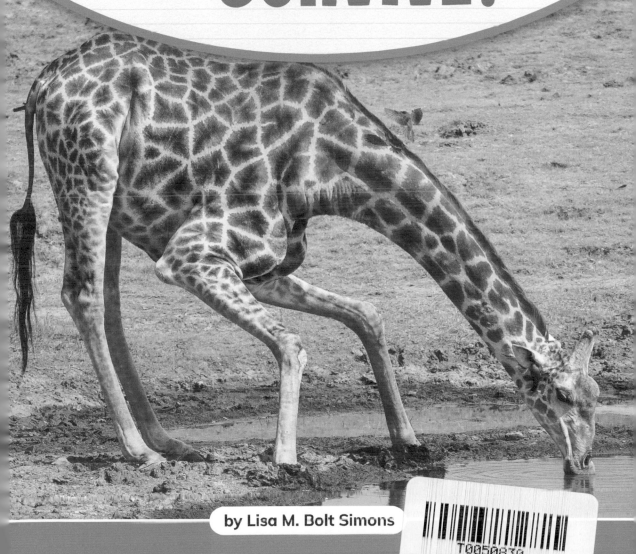

by Lisa M. Bolt Simons

PEBBLE
a capstone imprint

Pebble Explore is published by Pebble, an imprint of Capstone.
1710 Roe Crest Drive
North Mankato, Minnesota 56003
www.capstonepub.com

Library of Congress Cataloging-in-Publication Data
Names: Simons, Lisa M. B., 1969- author.
Title: What do animals need to survive? / by Lisa M. Bolt Simons.
Description: North Mankato, Minnesota : Pebble, [2022] | Series: Science inquiry | Includes bibliographical references and index. | Audience: Ages 5-8 | Audience: Grades 2-3 | Summary: "Animals are living things. They need certain things to grow and live. What are they? Let's investigate what animals need to survive!"— Provided by publisher.
Identifiers: LCCN 2021002877 (print) | LCCN 2021002878 (ebook) | ISBN 9781977131430 (hardcover) | ISBN 9781977132604 (paperback) | ISBN 9781977155283 (pdf) | ISBN 9781977156907 (kindle edition)
Subjects: LCSH: Physiology—Juvenile literature. | Animals—Juvenile literature. | Life (Biology)—Juvenile literature. | Habitat (Ecology)—Juvenile literature.
Classification: LCC QP31.2 .S54 2022 (print) | LCC QP31.2 (ebook) | DDC 591—dc23
LC record available at https://lccn.loc.gov/2021002877
LC ebook record available at https://lccn.loc.gov/2021002878

Image Credits
iStockphoto/FatCamera, 5 (top); Newscom/Wothe, K./picturealliance/Arco Images G, 27; Shutterstock: Adrian Eugen Ciobaniuc, 24, Agarianna76, 15, Aijintai, 19 (rabbit), Andrey Pavlov, 19 (ant), AnujinM, 19 (deer), ANURAK PONGPATIMET, 7 (middle right), Bachkova Natalia, 13, 25, Cathy Keifer, 20, Chase Dekker, 29, Crazy nook, 7 (bottom right), 9, Dennis Jacobsen, 21, Dora Zett, 7 (middle), Eric Isselee, 19 (bear, owl, snake, lion), fivespots, 19 (turtle), FloridaStock, 19 (eagle), hilton, 22, in the Open, 1, 17, Ivdonata, 23, Jakinnboaz, 11, Janelle Lugge, cover, Jim Cumming, 19 (fox), Jirik V, 5 (bottom), Kontrastwerk, 10, MyImages-Micha, 7 (top, bottom left), ronstik, 7 (middle left), Rudmer Zwerver, 19, Villiers Steyn, 12, yingtustocker, 19

Artistic elements: Shutterstock/balabolka

Editorial Credits
Editor: Erika L. Shores; Designers: Dina Her and Juliette Peters; Media Researcher: Kelly Garvin; Production Specialist: Tori Abraham

All internet sites appearing in back matter were available and accurate when this book was sent to press.

TABLE OF CONTENTS

Words in **bold** are in the glossary.

A SURVIVAL INVESTIGATION

You just got a new pet! Maybe it's a kitten. Maybe it's a turtle.

There are things you may want for your animal. Maybe you want to add rocks to your turtle's tank. Maybe you want a toy for your kitten. But the animals don't need those things to live. What do the animals need to grow strong and healthy?

All animals need four things to survive. What do you think these four things are?

Let's do an investigation to figure out what animals need. Look at the photos on page 7. Your new pet is a kitten. These photos are things on your shopping list.

Make **observations**. Look carefully and gather information.

Which of these things would help the kitten grow? Which of these things is a place for the kitten to sleep? What is the one thing that is missing? What does your kitten need that you can't buy?

You can't buy air! But animals need air, or oxygen, to breathe. Animals cannot stay alive without oxygen.

The other three things animals need are food, water, and shelter. Your kitten needs food. One photo shows kitten food. It will eat cat food when it grows up. Your kitten needs water to drink. Your kitten also needs shelter. It needs a place to live where it feels safe.

WHY IS AIR NEEDED FOR SURVIVAL?

Now you know the four things animals need to survive. But why? Let's explore a bit more.

Animals that are **vertebrates** and live on land have lungs. **Amphibians** like frogs have lungs too. But in water they also breathe through their skin.

Breathing

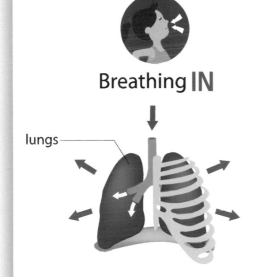

Breathing **IN**

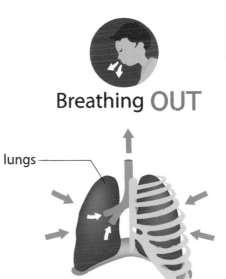

Breathing **OUT**

Animals breathe in oxygen, just like people do. The lungs fill up. Blood cells pick up the oxygen. It's carried through the body in the blood. Then animals breathe out **carbon dioxide**. Then the cycle repeats.

HOW IS WATER IMPORTANT FOR SURVIVAL?

Besides oxygen, animals need water. Animals can live without food for a long time. A few kinds of animals can go without food for months or even years! But most animals can only live without water for days.

Water is important for many reasons. Water helps animals control their body temperature. It's important that animals don't get too hot or too cold. If that happens, their bodies don't work normally. They can get very tired and sick.

Water also helps move things in the body. Blood has a lot of water. It can easily move through the body, or **circulate**.

When animals eat, water is important. Saliva in the mouth is mostly water. It can break down the food so animals can swallow it. Water also helps break down the food even more in the stomach.

Water then helps carry the food's vitamins and **nutrients** throughout the body. The vitamins and nutrients give the animals energy.

Animals also need water to get rid of waste. Waste is left over from food that the body doesn't need. Water helps the waste leave the body.

Water is important for another reason. Vertebrates have bones. Between some bones is bendy, flexible tissue called cartilage. It helps stop the bones from rubbing together. Cartilage needs water. It is important in joints, such as knees and elbows.

WHAT FOOD DO ANIMALS EAT TO SURVIVE?

When we think of animals, we mostly think of vertebrates. They are fish, reptiles, amphibians, birds, and **mammals**. Animals without backbones are called invertebrates. All animals are grouped into three types of eaters. They are **carnivores**, **herbivores**, and **omnivores**.

Think about your kitten. Its food is usually made of meat, such as chicken, and grains, such as rice. What kind of eater is your kitten?

carnivores

omnivores

herbivores

Animals that eat meat are called carnivores. Carnivores that hunt are called **predators**. Eagles and most spiders are predators.

The world's largest animal is the blue whale. It's a carnivore. It eats krill, which look like tiny shrimp.

Many carnivores are scavengers. Scavengers look for dead animals to eat. Vultures wait for animals to die. Wolves will eat dead animals other predators leave behind.

Herbivores are animals that mostly eat plants. Insects are tiny herbivores. There are huge herbivores like rhinoceroses and elephants.

Bees are herbivores. They help plants make new plants as they eat pollen and nectar, flying from flower to flower.

Earthworms are herbivores. They find dead plants to eat in soil.

The last kind of eater is an omnivore. That's us! Most mammals like your kitten, most birds, and some insects are omnivores.

Omnivores eat all sorts of food. Omnivores eat plants, such as fruits and vegetables. Omnivores eat animals, such as chickens. An omnivore might eat eggs and milk. These foods also come from animals.

WHY IS SHELTER IMPORTANT FOR SURVIVAL?

Think about your kitten. It lives inside your house. The kitten isn't hunted by wild animals. Shelter helps animals stay safe from predators.

Your kitten stays warm and dry inside your house too. Wild animals need shelter from the weather.

Animals also need shelter to have their young. Animals that lay eggs need safe places for a nest. Animals that give birth need safe places for their young to grow.

Sometimes when animals build shelters, new shelters are made for other animals. For example, beavers build dams. The dams can cause ponds to form. Animals use the ponds for their new homes.

Animals need four things to survive. They need shelter to stay safe. Food gives animals energy. Water is even more important than food. But air is the most important of all. In our homes or in the wild, animals need those four things to live.

GLOSSARY

amphibian (am-FI-bee-uhn)—an animal that lives in water when it is young and on land as an adult; some amphibians, such as frogs, can live in water and on land as adults

carbon dioxide (KAHR-buhn dahy-OK-sid)—a colorless gas released into the air when animals breathe out or exhale

carnivore (KAHR-nuh-vawr)—an animal that eats other animals

circulate (SUR-kyuh-leyt)—to move around in a course from beginning to end

herbivore (HUR-buh-vawr)—an animal that eats plants

mammal (MAM-uhl)—a warm–blooded animal that breathes air and has hair or fur; female mammals feed milk to their young

nutrient (NOO-tree-uhnt)—substance or matter that is healthy

observation (ob-zur-VEY-shuhn)—to make note about what is seen or noticed

omnivore (OM-nuh-vawr)—an animal that eats both other animals and plants

predator (PRED-uh-ter)—an animal that hunts and kills other animals to survive

vertebrate (VUR-tuh-brit)—an animal with a backbone

READ MORE

Lindeen, Mary. *What Animals Need*. Chicago: Norwood House Press, 2019.

Rice, Dona Herweck. *Where Are the Animals?* Huntington Beach, CA: Teacher Created Materials, 2019.

Sohn, Emily and Barbara J. Foster. *Animal Needs*. Chicago: Norwood House Press. 2020.

INTERNET SITES

Animal Needs
youtube.com/watch?v=Pe9kSlVeEIM

Biology for Kids: Breathing and the Respiratory System
ducksters.com/science/breathing.php

Needs of Animals—Food and Shelter
youtube.com/watch?v=53VIgf5mtn0

INDEX